# ALL ABOUT MEASURING

# VOLUME

Julia Vogel

# LET'S READ
## AV² BY WEIGL™
### ADDED VALUE • AUDIO VISUAL

Go to **www.av2books.com**, and enter this book's unique code.

## BOOK CODE

C924829

**AV² by Weigl** brings you media enhanced books that support active learning.

AV² provides enriched content that supplements and complements this book. Weigl's AV² books strive to create inspired learning and engage young minds in a total learning experience.

## Your AV² Media Enhanced books come alive with...

**Audio**
Listen to sections of the book read aloud.

**Video**
Watch informative video clips.

**Embedded Weblinks**
Gain additional information for research.

**Try This!**
Complete activities and hands-on experiments.

**Key Words**
Study vocabulary, and complete a matching word activity.

**Quizzes**
Test your knowledge.

**Slide Show**
View images and captions, and prepare a presentation.

## ... and much, much more!

Published by AV² by Weigl
350 5th Avenue, 59th Floor New York, NY 10118
Website: www.av2books.com

Library of Congress Control Number: 2016956796

ISBN 978-1-4896-5881-4 (hardcover)
ISBN 978-1-4896-5882-1 (softcover)
ISBN 978-1-4896-5883-8 (multi-user eBook)

Printed in the United States of America in Brainerd, Minnesota
1 2 3 4 5 6 7 8 9 0   20 19 18 17 16

122016
121616

Project Coordinator: Piper Whelan
Art Director: Terry Paulhus

Every reasonable effort has been made to trace ownership and to obtain permission to reprint copyright material. The publisher would be pleased to have any errors or omissions brought to its attention so that they may be corrected in subsequent printings.

The publisher acknowledges iStock and Alamy as the primary image suppliers for this title.

# CONTENTS

# What is Volume?

Have you ever asked, "How much?" How much medicine do you take when you are sick? How much milk goes in the brownies? How much water fills the backyard pool?

How can you find the answers? By measuring volume! Volume is the amount of space something takes up.

In baking, recipes call for different amounts of ingredients. This helps the food to taste good.

# Estimating Volume

Long ago, people did not use exact measures of volume. They learned from practice how much water to put in the soup. They also learned how much wheat made a loaf of bread. They used clay pots, baskets, or handfuls to estimate amounts.

But pots and baskets were not all the same. People needed standard units to measure volume. This way everyone would get the same answers when they measured the same things.

## Estimate It

How much is a handful?
Take a plastic bowl to a
sink. Turn on the water.
Cup your hands and catch
a handful. Count how
many handfuls of water
it takes to fill the bowl.
Pour the water out and
try again. Did you get the
same count both times?

A gallon jug of milk has 16 cups of milk in it.

# Measuring Liquids

Since the 1800s, people in the United States have used the gallon unit to measure volumes of liquid. Apple cider, milk, and laundry detergent are often sold in gallon jugs. One gallon jug holds 1 gallon of liquid.

Let's say you have a bucket of water. You want to see how much water is in the bucket. You can use a funnel to pour it into a gallon jug. Does it all fit? The volume of the water is 1 gallon or less. Do you have water leftover when the jug is full? Your bucket has more than 1 gallon.

What if the water does not fill the jug? How can you measure how much water you have? You need to use smaller units. The U.S. customary system has several units smaller than a gallon.

You may have seen a quart of juice in your refrigerator or a pint of ice cream in your freezer. A quart is one-fourth the size of a gallon. That means it would take 4 quarts to make 1 gallon. A pint is one-eighth the size of a gallon.

You can pour the water from the bucket into these containers. Then you can see if you have about a quart or a pint.

Mason jars are used for canning food. They come in half-pint, pint, quart, and half-gallon sizes.

What if the water doesn't fill those containers? You'll need even smaller units. Cups might work. One cup is half as much as a pint or one-fourth as much as a quart. Sixteen cups make 1 gallon.

Use a measuring cup to measure the water in your bucket. Count each cup of water you scoop out. You can place each cup in a separate bowl.

# Adding and Subtracting

Make sure you keep track of units when doing math. Two plus two does not equal four if you're adding 2 gallons and 2 pints. Remember, you have to add or subtract numbers with the same units.

Cooks and parents need even smaller units. They might measure a liquid in ounces. Eight ounces make 1 cup. Look at the label on a bottle of cooking oil. How many ounces are inside?

A tablespoon is even smaller than an ounce. There are 2 tablespoons in 1 ounce. There are 3 teaspoons in 1 tablespoon. You might know these units from taking medicine.

# Measuring Spoons

A set of measuring spoons has spoons even smaller than teaspoons. There may be a one-half teaspoon and a one-fourth teaspoon. Those spoons hold a tiny bit. But cooks know that a tiny amount of some flavors is plenty.

# The Metric System

What a lot of units! The U.S. customary system can be confusing. Most of the world uses another system. It is the metric system. In this system, the basic unit for volume is the liter. People in Europe buy liters of apple cider instead of gallons. One liter is just a bit more than 1 quart.

# Liters and Milliliters

Liter units are easy to work with. They are easily divided into smaller units. When doctors give medicine, they often use milliliters. There are about 5 milliliters in 1 teaspoon of medicine.

Most blueberries are sold in pint-sized packages.

# Measuring Solids

Solids can be measured by volume, too. A farmer's market is a good place to learn about the volume of dry solids. You can buy a pint of blueberries and a quart of peas. You can also buy a peck of apples and a bushel of potatoes. Even bigger amounts are a hogshead of sugar and a cord of wood.

# What Equals What?

Confused by all the different units?
Here's a list to help keep them straight.

1 bushel = 4 pecks

1 peck = 2 gallons

1 gallon = 4 quarts

1 quart = 2 pints

1 pint = 2 cups

1 cup = 8 ounces

1 ounce = 2 tablespoons

1 tablespoon = 3 teaspoons

Different types of measuring tools are needed for baking and cooking.

8 CUPS — 2 QTS.

6 — 1 1/2 QTS.

4 — 1 QT.

2 — 1 PT.

8 OZ.

1/8 Tsp

# Measuring Mania

Now you can answer questions by measuring volume. You can answer how much medicine, milk, or water you need in teaspoons, liters, and more.

What other questions can you answer? Grab your measuring cups and start measuring!

Many measuring tools have labels for both cups and ounces.

# KEY WORDS

Research has shown that as much as 65 percent of all written material published in English is made up of 300 words. These 300 words cannot be taught using pictures or learned by sounding them out. They must be recognized by sight. This book contains 112 common sight words to help young readers improve their reading fluency and comprehension. This book also teaches young readers several important content words, such as proper nouns. These words are paired with pictures to aid in learning and improve understanding.

| Page | Sight Words First Appearance |
|------|------------------------------|
| 4 | answer, are, asked, by, can, do, find, have, how, in, is, much, of, something, take, the, up, water, when, you |
| 5 | call, different, food, for, good, help, this, to |
| 6 | all, also, and, but, did, from, get, long, made, not, or, people, put, same, they, things, use, way, were, would |
| 7 | a, again, both, hand, it, many, on, out, try, your |
| 8 | has |
| 9 | does, into, let, more, often, one, say, see, than, want |
| 10 | about, if, make, may, means, need, that, then, these, what |
| 11 | as, come |
| 12 | each, even, might, place, those, work |
| 13 | add, four, keep, two, with |
| 14 | an, at, know, look, there |
| 15 | be, set, some |
| 16 | another, just, most, world |
| 17 | give |
| 19 | learn, too |
| 20 | here, list, them |
| 22 | now, other |

| Page | Content Words First Appearance |
|------|--------------------------------|
| 4 | brownies, medicine, milk, pool, volume |
| 5 | ingredients, recipes |
| 6 | baskets, bread, clay pots, soup, wheat |
| 7 | bowl, cup, handful |
| 8 | gallon, jug |
| 9 | apple cider, bucket, laundry detergent, United States |
| 10 | containers, freezer, ice cream, juice, pint, quart, refrigerator, U.S. customary system |
| 11 | Mason jars |
| 14 | bottle, cooks, ounces, parents, tablespoon, teaspoons |
| 16 | Europe, liters, metric system |
| 17 | doctors, milliliters |
| 18 | blueberries |
| 19 | farmer's market, peas, potatoes, sugar, wood |

## Check out www.av2books.com for activities, videos, audio clips, and more!

1 Go to www.av2books.com.

2 Enter book code.  C924829

3 Fuel your imagination online!

www.av2books.com